Religious Freedom

Sean Connolly

A+

Smart Apple Media

Published by Smart Apple Media
2140 Howard Drive West, North Mankato, MN 56003

Design and production by Helen James

Photographs by Corbis (Fernando Alda, Paul Almasy, Archivo Iconografico, S.A.,
Bettmann, Bohan Brecelj, Burstein Collection, Pablo Corral V, Kevin Fleming,
HUDSON DEREK/CORBIS SYGMA, Hulton–Deutsch Collection, Andrea Jemolo,
Bob Krist, William Manning, Francis G. Mayer, Mary Ann McDonald, Franklin McMahon,
Jean–Paul Pelissier/Reuters, Mark Peterson, Chris Rainier, Reuters, Leonard de Selva,
David H. Wells, ZAHID HUSSEIN/Reuters), Getty Images (Spencer Platt)

Library of Congress Cataloging-in-Publication Data

Connolly, Sean.
Religious freedom / by Sean Connolly.
p. cm. — (Campaigns for change)
Includes bibliographical references and index.
ISBN 1-58340-514-3
1. Freedom of religion—History—Juvenile literature. I. Title. II. Series.

BL640.C66 2005
323.44'2—dc22   2004051207

First Edition

9 8 7 6 5 4 3 2 1

Contents

Freedom to Believe

From the earliest times, human beings have drawn comfort and a sense of belonging from their religious beliefs. These beliefs have differed over time and from place to place, but they have remained an important part of most societies. And although today most people consider religion to be a matter of individual choice,

Wall paintings in a cave near Rusape, Zimbabwe, show that humans were concerned with spiritual matters even before they had written languages.

whole cultures have been divided over the issue of religion. Even more tragically, some of the worst hatred and violence in history has been between people whose religious beliefs share the same basic message of peace, love, and tolerance.

Peace and Division

Followers of three of the major world religions—Judaism, Christianity, and **Islam**—are often called "people of the book" because they all believe that the words of the Bible are sacred. Being people of the book has not stopped Christians in 19th-century Russia or 20th-century Germany from killing their Jewish neighbors. Nor has it prevented **Muslims** and Christians from fighting each other since the time of the first **Crusades** more than 1,000 years ago. Somewhere along the line, the peaceful message that underpins most of the world's religions has been lost for some people. Instead of seeing the things they have in common with—or could learn from—believers of other religions, they consider them enemies who are trying to destroy the true faith.

Brigid of Kildare, a sixth-century Irish saint, reads the Bible. Religion has been a source of both pride and division in Ireland.

This sad byproduct of religious belief seems to have as long a history as religion itself. It has turned some people away from religion altogether. But it has driven others to search for a way for worshipers of all faiths to hold their beliefs in peace, even if those beliefs differ from the beliefs of their neighbors. Religious freedom—the right of individuals to believe as their conscience dictates—is a goal for these people. Some countries, including the United States, have included this goal in their **constitutions**, while others have developed less formal systems that allow for religious variety. But in some countries, religious freedom is still a long way from being reality.

Choosing Unity Over Division

The area of southern Asia that includes India and Persia (modern Iran) produced many of the oldest religions in the world. Hinduism, **Buddhism**, and Zoroastrianism all took root in this region thousands of years ago. Over time, rivalries arose among these religions and with new faiths, such as Christianity and Islam, which arrived from the west and found new **converts**. These conflicts, especially between the Hindu and Muslim populations of India, have led to thousands of deaths over the years and continue to this day.

This same region, however, has also produced two religions that have tried to find the principles that unite—rather than divide—worshipers of different faiths. Sikhism was founded by the Indian Nanak (1469–1539), who took elements of Hinduism and Islam to develop a new religion. Sikhs believe that there is a single God who overcomes all religious distinctions. About 400 years later, a similar message appeared in Persia. Another man, named Bahaullah, proclaimed himself to be the latest in a series of heavenly-inspired prophets who included the Buddha, Jesus Christ, and Muhammad (founder of the Islamic faith). Followers of Bahaullah's teachings describe their religion as the Baha'i faith. These two religions continue to thrive and to find new converts around the world.

Sikh boys, wearing the traditional turbans of their faith, study at a London school in the mid-1990s.

Freedom to Believe

Keeping Pace With the Times

Religious leaders and believers have often seized new methods of communication to share their message. The invention of the printing press in the 16th century offered an oppurtunity to spread the word of the Bible to anyone who wanted to read it. Until then, the only copies of the Bible were produced painstakingly by hand. As a result, the few existing copies were in the hands of the clergy and the very rich.

Similarly, Christian preachers grasped the power of first radio, then television, in the 20th century. The most popular ministers found themselves with congregations in the millions, rather than the hundreds. The next step has been into the "virtual world" of the Internet, where thousands of Web sites spread the word about—and in some cases, against—various religious denominations.

Jim and Tammy Faye Bakker produced one of the most popular religious television programs in the United States before some viewers began criticizing their rich lifestyle.

"No man [should] be compelled to frequent or support any religious worship, place, or ministry whatsoever, nor [should he] . . . otherwise suffer on account of his religious opinions or belief."

From the Virginia **Statute** for Religious Freedom, drafted by Thomas Jefferson in 1779.

Mutual Respect

It is easy for people in the 21st century to believe that their lives, and the societies in which they live, are more advanced than those that went before them. People can look at the material accomplishments—supersonic planes, cell phones, and laptop computers—and compare them with horse-drawn carriages, oil lamps, and quill pens. The conclusion seems obvious: the modern world is a more advanced place than the ancient world.

It is just as easy to assume that many of the human rights that modern people cherish—such as racial and gender equality, freedom of speech, and workplace safety—are also recent achievements and that earlier societies had nothing of the sort. But a close look at history shows that, in many ways, some older (and even ancient) civilizations promoted justice and liberty, including religious freedom, in ways that some modern societies can only dream about.

A Shinto monk visits a shrine on Mount Hoguro. Shinto is an ancient Japanese religion that has survived the arrival—and at times, blended with—other religions such as Buddhism, Confucianism, and Christianity.

Might and Right

In ancient times, it was common for powerful nations to overrun and conquer their neighbors. The victors would often destroy temples and other places of worship, imposing their own system of religion on the defeated people. The saying "might makes right," meaning that the powerful can decide right and wrong (including in religious matters), refers to this practice. Even in countries that weren't conquered, religions often grew in much the same way. The people of the country were forced to follow the religious beliefs of a powerful ruler, such as an Egyptian pharaoh, whose word was law.

Some mighty countries, however, showed that they could remain powerful while allowing other faiths to thrive and develop. More than 1,000 years ago, Japan developed its **Shinto** religion, which raised the emperor to the level of a god. But the Japanese allowed beliefs from other regions—Buddhism from India and **Confucianism** from China, for example—to exist alongside the Shinto religion.

It was even more important for larger countries—those that went on to create empires—to consider the beliefs of the people they conquered. The ancient Romans developed a religion based on sacrifices made to dozens of gods. But as Rome conquered more lands, the Roman government legally acknowledged

The fifth-century B.C. Roman temple of Neptune at Paestum, Italy, is evidence that the Romans borrowed the architectural style—as well as many of the religious beliefs—from the Greeks.

The mosque at Cordoba, built in A.D. 786, is one of the treasures left from the 700-year rule of the Moors in Spain.

"If I were to see among the race of women another who is so remarkable a woman as this, I would say that the race of women is superior to the race of men."

A 13th-century Arab doctor, referring to the religious and cultural accomplishments of Sorghaghtani Beki within the Mongol Empire.

other religions. Judaism was one such religion, and some of the first Christians played up their Jewish connections to benefit from this legal protection. Christianity itself became the official religion of the Roman Empire in the fourth century A.D. after Emperor Constantine converted to the faith and prohibited all other religions.

One of the "golden periods" of European culture was linked to the 700-year Muslim rule of Spain, lasting until the end of the 15th century. At a time when other European regions were mired in the Dark Ages, Spain was enjoying a period of civilization and learning. The Moors (as the Spanish called the Muslims) invited scholars from around the known world to discuss philosophy, medicine, and science. Muslims, Jews, and Christians lived and worked side by side. Non-Muslims at that time were free to practice their own religions. The only restriction they faced was a little extra tax.

Mongol Wisdom

Beginning under the leadership of the famous soldier Genghis Khan, the Mongols swept from their Asian homeland to create the largest land empire the world has ever seen. At its height in the 13th century, the Mongol Empire covered nearly 14 million square miles (36 million sq km) and included more than 100 million people. It stretched from the Pacific coast westward across Asia and as far as Russia and Hungary. Mongol horsemen, riding bareback and with light armor, were among the most feared fighters in the world. The khan, or ruler of the Mongols, inspired loyalty and strict obedience among these troops.

Despite the Mongols' terrifying military reputation, the empire they created relied on cooperation and understanding, rather than brute force. Genghis's daughter-in-law (and mother of the equally famous Kublai Khan), Sorghaghtani Beki, knew that it would be impossible to rule such a large and varied empire without a knowledge of the people within it. While she herself never ruled, she had enormous influence over the upbringing of her four sons and made sure that each learned a different foreign language that he could

use in ruling. She also made sure that influential Mongols studied to become leaders in the different religions of the empire, including Confucianism (in China), Hinduism (in southern Asia), and Islam (in southwestern Asia). Religious tolerance became the official law, and every religion was supported across the empire. Believers appreciated this merciful approach, and, with it, the Mongols were able to eliminate a possible source of conflict within the empire.

This 15th-century Mongol work uses Arabic to illustrate an episode in Islamic history.

A Church Divided

Religious freedom was rarely practiced during the **Middle Ages** in Europe. Most western Europeans belonged to the Roman Catholic Church, so there was little reason to consider the needs of other believers. Jewish people lived in relative peace in many European countries, although from time to time, local Christian populations would turn on them with violent attacks.

Differences of opinion within the Church were normally resolved peacefully. Responding to charges that the Church had become too concerned with wealth, medieval popes established new religious orders such as the Franciscans and Dominicans. Their example of poverty and devotion helped sway European Christians away from beliefs that the Church considered **heresies**. When exemplary behavior and preaching were not enough, these orders played a part in the Inquisition, a religious court that aimed to crush religious opposition.

The Spanish Inquisition unleashed a world of terror in the name of Christianity. This scene from 1492 shows the burning of Jews who refused to accept the Catholic faith of their rulers.

The Inquisition could be cruel and pitiless in its decisions, especially in the way it dealt with Jews and Muslims in 15th-century Spain. Many were tortured to force them to convert to Catholicism; those who refused lost their property and were expelled from Spain.

The most groundbreaking Christian development came with the **Reformation**, which began when Martin Luther, a German monk, publicized his protests against the Catholic Church in 1517. Luther soon found many followers who, like himself, were prepared to depart from the Catholic Church. These Christians became known as Protestants.

Hearts and Minds

Although many different Protestant **denominations** developed, most thought that each believer should be able to look to the Bible for inspiration and salvation. This individual approach was different from that of the Catholic Church. With the pope as the most important religious leader, the Catholic Church taught that worshipers should trust the Church itself to interpret the Bible.

As European rulers chose either the Catholic or Protestant faith, their followers began to fight one another. Religious differences developed into political and military conflict. Throughout much of the 16th century, France was torn apart by religious wars between Catholic and Protestant groups. Peace came only when Henri IV became king in 1589. A Protestant who became a Catholic in order to gain the throne, Henri was in a good position to understand viewpoints on both sides of the conflict. In 1598, he issued the Edict of Nantes

Martin Luther, depicted in this 1533 painting by German artist Lucas Cranach the Elder, paved the way for new forms of Christian worship, but these new freedoms also provoked violent divisions in Europe.

(see page 15), one of the earliest and most important guarantees of religious freedom in the modern world.

What Sort of Freedom?

Throughout this period of turmoil, rival Christian groups fought for the freedom to practice their faith. They often took up arms to force their case, and the victorious group often denied religious freedom to other Christians, sometimes even executing those who did not share their religious beliefs.

England provides a good example. After King Henry VIII of England parted with the Roman Catholic Church to form the Church of England in 1529, Catholics found their freedoms limited. These limitations became more intense after Henry's death in 1547. The Church of England became more Protestant during

the brief reign of King Edward VI, with Catholics finding it hard to get government jobs or find places to worship freely. The king's half sister Mary became queen when Edward died in 1553. Mary I was a Catholic and did everything in her power to overturn the work of Henry and Edward. Almost 300 English Protestants were burned as **heretics** during Mary's five-year reign, and many English people still refer to her as "Bloody Mary." England regained its religious peace under the reign of Queen Elizabeth I, who ruled from 1558 to 1603. The Church of England returned as the national religion, but Elizabeth tried to make her changes with compromise rather than violence.

England saw its first wide-scale religious violence during the reign of Queen Mary in the mid-16th century. Hundreds of Protestants died as she tried to restore the Catholic faith in her country.

The Edict of Nantes

The Wars of Religion that tore France apart in the 16th century were violent and bloody. Catholics and Huguenots (French Protestants) fought each other for control of France—and, with it, the chance to impose their beliefs on the entire country. The worst episode in this terrible conflict was the St. Bartholomew's Day Massacre on August 24, 1572. Catholic rioters rampaged through Paris, murdering thousands of Huguenots. It became clear to both sides that similar outbreaks would become common unless some sort of peace was imposed on the country.

Huguenots faced a fiery death during the most violent episodes of the religious wars that rocked France during the 16th century.

That peace came when Henri of Navarre, a skilled Huguenot military leader, was in a position to become King of France in 1589. Most French people were still Catholic, so Henri converted to their faith as a gesture of peace. Once he became king, though, Henri ensured that Huguenots were able to practice their faith freely by issuing the Edict of Nantes in 1598. The country benefited from this legally granted settlement, although over the next 90 years, Protestants began to face restrictions once again. The Edict of Nantes was overturned in 1685, causing as many as 400,000 Huguenots to leave France for more welcoming places, including the colonies that would later become the United States.

The Jesuits

With wars of religion brewing in the 16th century, it is not surprising that the most famous Catholic order formed at that time was organized along military-style lines, with senior members able to issue orders to others in the same way that military officers ordered their men. The Society of Jesus (its members are called Jesuits) was approved by Pope Paul III in 1540. Its original purpose was to convert Muslims in the Holy Land to Catholicism. But the upheaval caused by the Reformation led Jesuits to concentrate on "winning back" those countries that had chosen the Protestant faith. They set up colleges in Catholic countries where Catholics from Protestant countries could go to strengthen their faith. These Jesuit-educated Catholics would then return to their Protestant home countries, such as England, Scotland, and Sweden, to carry on the cause.

Jesuits who entered Protestant countries had to travel in secret since they were constantly followed by spies and informers. If caught, they faced torture or execution. John Ogilvie, a Scottish Jesuit, was sentenced to death by a Glasgow court in 1615. He was hanged, and his body was mutilated to intimidate others who might follow his example.

A Silver Lining

With people being persecuted or even killed for their religious beliefs, there seemed little reason for hope in the 16th and 17th centuries. But it gradually became clear that forcing people away from their countries was bad political policy. Many of the hundreds of thousands of Huguenots who fled from France sought refuge in Britain and in the British colonies of North America. Britain traditionally had been an enemy of France, and the new arrivals helped strengthen British businesses—to the disadvantage of France. Although the Huguenots rarely joined the Church of England, the British tolerated their different religious opinions because of the economic contribution made by the French arrivals.

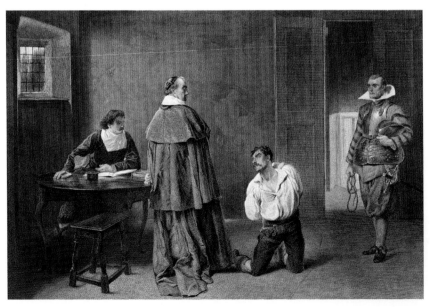

A Huguenot kneels at the center of this engraving, awaiting his punishment. Distressing scenes like this led many Huguenots to flee their native France in favor of lands that offered more religious freedom.

Anabaptists

One early Protestant group held beliefs that led to conflict with other Protestant leaders. These people were the Anabaptists, whose name comes from the belief that only adults can make the decision to be baptized. Anabaptists also believed that there should be no national churches at a time when Europe was divided into Catholic and Protestant national religions. This belief, along with their unwillingness to take part in any sort of government, even by voting, led the Anabaptists into violent conflict with others.

Despite opposition, many Anabaptist groups developed in different parts of Europe and America. One such group was the Mennonites, many of whom left the religious turmoil of Europe to settle in North America from the 17th century onward. The Amish people of Pennsylvania and other states are a Mennonite group that has carried on the traditions—and even the fashions—of those first Mennonite settlers. Over the years, however, the Amish and other Mennonites have had to battle to remain separate from the other Americans living around them. In 1972, for example, the U.S. Supreme Court allowed an Amish family in Wisconsin to remove their children from local public schools after the eighth grade even though Wisconsin law states that children must remain in school until they are 16. The Supreme Court agreed that staying in school would make it hard for the children to carry on traditional Amish customs. In the end, the family's freedom of religion was more important than the legal requirement to stay in school.

Three Mennonite girls walk along a rural Pennsylvania road in the 1980s, wearing clothes that would not look out of place centuries earlier.

New World, New Freedom?

By the early 17th century, several European countries had begun to form colonies in North and South America, or the "New World," as they called it. The vast lands opening up for them in the Americas offered European nations a chance to expand and become more powerful. Abundant natural resources, especially the promise of gold and silver, hinted at the wealth that could be gained by establishing a foothold across the Atlantic.

France, Spain, and Portugal sent settlers who were loyal to both their kings and their countries' Catholic faith. Priests and nuns accompanied soldiers, fur trappers, and other settlers to the Americas. Many Protestant European countries, such as Sweden and the Netherlands, took a different approach. They granted individuals the chance to establish colonies in the monarch's name in return for the opportunity to make money for themselves by making the colonies successful. Virginia (named after Elizabeth I, England's "Virgin Queen") was one such colony.

A priest from the Church of England baptizes Virginia Dare in 1587. She was the first child to be born of English parents in North America.

Native Americans offer Roger Williams a symbolic peace pipe in this painting of Williams's arrival in Rhode Island in 1636.

Breakthrough in Rhode Island

Roger Williams was an English clergyman who settled in the Massachusetts Bay Colony, which was governed by **Puritans**. Williams began to clash with Massachusetts's leaders almost as soon as he arrived. He claimed that the charter of Massachusetts did not allow its leaders to impose any type of religion on its settlers. He also argued that the colony had no right to take land from the local Native Americans; he maintained that the Native Americans had to sell these lands freely.

In 1636, Williams escaped punishment from Massachusetts authorities and moved south into what is now Rhode Island. There he bought land from the Narragansett tribe of Native Americans and established the colony of Rhode Island. Unlike Massachusetts, Rhode Island offered complete religious toleration and separation of church and state, two ideas that would later become cornerstones of the United States. Rhode Island attracted persecuted believers from the beginning. America's first Baptist church was built in Providence in 1639, and in 1658, a group of Spanish and Portuguese Jews established a settlement in Newport. The 1663 Charter of Rhode Island guaranteed the rights that would later become accepted and admired throughout North America.

The Touro Synagogue, built in Newport, Rhode Island, in 1763, is the oldest synagogue in the U.S.—evidence of the long tradition of religious freedom in Rhode Island.

Other English colonies, however, were formed by religious "troublemakers" who left their home country. The Pilgrims, who formed a colony at Plymouth, Massachusetts, were **Separatists** who had split from the Church of England. Pennsylvania was founded by William Penn, a prominent Quaker (another Protestant group that questioned the Church of England). The first English settlers in Maryland were Catholics who sought a place where they could practice their religion freely.

Turning the Tables

Compared with Spanish, French, and Portuguese colonies, which all had the Catholic faith imposed on them, English colonies offered a wide variety of religious beliefs. **Dissenters** and **Anglicans** alike could find a colony where they could worship. But in many ways, religious freedom was as limited as it had been in the "Old World." Catholics were not welcomed except in Maryland (which eventually gained a Protestant majority). And the strict beliefs of the Pilgrims and Puritans of New England did not allow for any real disagreement. Those who questioned the system of church organization in New England were punished or driven away. The new colonists had been able to find their own freedom of worship, but they rarely extended it to others.

"God requireth not a **uniformity** of religion to be enacted and enforced in any civil state; which . . . (sooner or later) is the greatest occasion of civil war, **ravishing** of conscience, **persecution** of Christ Jesus in his servants, and of the hypocrisy and destruction of millions of souls."

Roger Williams, founder of the colony of Rhode Island.

20

Brotherly Love

William Penn (1644–1718) was an Englishman who helped pave the way for religious freedom in North America. Penn had become a Quaker as a young man, and his religious beliefs led to several jail sentences in England. While in prison in 1671, Penn wrote *The Great Cause of Liberty of Conscience*, a short work that supported religious toleration. Ten years later, Penn obtained a grant of territory in North America as part of a debt owed to his father. The following year, he established the colony of Pennsylvania, named for his father. Penn also founded a new city, which he called Philadelphia (Greek for "brotherly love").

Penn described his new settlement as the "Holy Experiment," and he promised religious toleration to all who came to live there. After governing for about two years, Penn returned to help Quakers living in England. Again, his religious convictions led him into conflict, as he faced charges of **treason** for his correspondence with the exiled Catholic King James II. Penn was cleared of the charges and returned to Pennsylvania in 1699 for two years. During that time, he issued the Charter of Privileges, a guarantee of religious freedom in the colony. This document inspired the U.S. founding fathers when they drafted the Constitution nearly a century later.

The 19th-century artist and Quaker preacher Edward Hicks took pleasure in depicting William Penn's friendly relations with the Native Americans of what would become Pennsylvania.

Revolutionary Beliefs

French artist Jean Jacques François LeBarbier gave a religious feel to his 1789 painting celebrating the Declaration of the Rights of Man, one of guiding documents of the French Revolution.

After the religious battles of the 16th and 17th centuries, the 18th century brought a new way of looking at life. Scientific discoveries had made many people believe that clear thinking and practical knowledge would be the best tools for improving life. Instead of relying on God to approve or disapprove of people's actions—and possibly step in to change things—some people proposed new ways of establishing fair and equitable systems. This period has been called the Enlightenment, because its followers believed that scientific discoveries lit the path toward human progress.

Putting Theory into Practice

Enlightenment thinkers published books and corresponded with each other throughout the 18th century. They called for new types of government that would offer people a greater say in running things, as well as more freedom of thought. By the end of the 1700s, they had a chance to make the changes they sought. **Revolutions** in the United States and France overthrew old systems of government and allowed people to start fresh.

Religious freedom was one of the goals of revolutionaries in both countries. In 1777, while the Revolutionary War was being fought in America, Thomas Jefferson drafted the

Constitutional Rights

When the United States became independent, it needed to establish a new government. It had to find a way for 13 states—which had been separate colonies under the British—to work as a single country. In 1787, representatives from the states met to define a governmental system for the new country. The resulting document, known as the U.S. Constitution, was then sent to each state to be approved.

The Constitution was in place when the first U.S. Congress met in 1789, but it faced more than 150 proposed amendments (changes or additions). Most of these amendments concerned individual liberties, since the Constitution had concentrated on systems of government. Eventually, Congress narrowed these amendments down to 12. Two of these proposals were voted down, but the other 10 became the first 10 amendments to the Constitution, known as the Bill of Rights. It is obvious how important religious freedom was to the members of the first Congress, because the First Amendment—which has been cited in hundreds of legal battles in U.S. history—states: "Congress shall make no laws respecting an establishment of religion, or prohibiting the free exercise thereof."

Thomas Jefferson's strong influence on the creation of the Bill of Rights is honored today at the Jefferson Memorial in Washington, D.C.

"I disagree with what you say, but I defend to the death your right to say it."

Voltaire, French philosopher whose ideas about freedom influenced ideas about religious liberty during the French Revolution.

Statute for Religious Freedom in his native Virginia. This document separated religion from government and guaranteed Virginians the right to worship as they pleased. The statute stated that "all men shall be free to profess, and by argument to maintain, their opinion in matters of religion." Jefferson ensured that the spirit of this law would be preserved nationally when the U.S. became independent by insisting that the U.S. Constitution guarantee religious freedom.

American statesman sign the U.S. Constitution in 1787, ensuring that their new country will guarantee basic rights such as freedom of religion.

France had produced many of the leading thinkers of the Enlightenment, including Jean Jacques Rousseau and Voltaire. The French system of government, with power resting in the hands of the king, the Catholic Church, and the wealthy, was the target of those who wanted change. In July 1789, protestors stormed the Bastille Prison in Paris, a symbol of the Old Regime. The French Revolution had begun. Although revolutionaries would eventually quarrel among themselves—and even execute many rivals—some of the basic goals of the Revolution remained unchanged. These goals were set out in August 1789 in a document known as the Declaration of the Rights of Man. This document enshrined the notions of equality and freedom—including religious freedom—that would become the cornerstones of the new French government.

Freedom or Toleration?

The American system guarantees and preserves religious "freedom," rather than "toleration." This freedom is based on the complete separation of a country's government from any form of religion. In matters of religion, citizens are free to believe—or not to believe—as they choose. Such a system requires a complete break from the ideas of government that underpinned European politics for centuries. It considers religious freedom to be a basic right, not a privilege to be granted or taken away by a government.

A system of religious toleration, on the other hand, is based on the idea that the government supports a particular religion (usually a Christian religion in European countries) but allows other forms of belief to exist. Religious toleration seemed to be the only way to solve the religious conflicts that divided Europe until the mid-17th century. The Treaty of Westphalia, which ended the **Thirty Years' War** in 1648, was one example. England's Act of Toleration (1689) was another. In these and other settlements, a particular type of religion continued to be official, although the government could choose to allow others to exist within the country.

Today, Scandinavian countries recognize the Protestant Lutheran faith as their official religion while tolerating other denominations. Spain and Italy, on the other hand, once recognized Catholicism as their official state religion, but in the late 20th century dropped its official status in favor of a system of complete religious freedom.

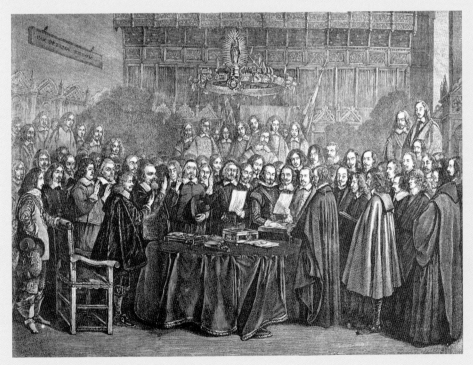

The signing of the Treaty of Westphalia marked a turning point in European history, guaranteeing religious tolerance and bringing to an end an era of religious conflicts.

Battling Old Values

Most countries in the 19th century had either resolved their religious differences or chosen to ignore them. New ideas, many based on the promise of wealth offered by the **Industrial Revolution**, took center stage. But behind the scenes, many people—especially European Jews—still faced discrimination and sometimes violence. This hidden persecution sometimes surfaced even in places where religious freedom had supposedly been achieved. The Dreyfus Affair (see page 27) in France pitted **anti-Semitic** forces against those who wanted to safeguard religious freedom. As with so many areas of social life during this period, the forces of progress still faced opposition in the field of religious freedom. As countries or their empires expanded, nations had to come to terms with people who held beliefs very different from Europe's traditional Christian and Jewish background.

Jewish people are expelled from Lithuania in 1844 during one of the bouts of violent anti-Semitism that marked European history.

"I Accuse"

Alfred Dreyfus, a French army officer of the Jewish faith, was arrested in 1893, charged with passing military secrets to the Germans. He was found guilty a year later and sentenced to life in prison on the notorious Devil's Island off the coast of South America. Many French people, including officials of the Catholic Church, used Dreyfus's conviction to condemn Jews living in France. Others, though, defended Dreyfus and Jewish people in general. They were helped by new evidence, which showed that another officer had been the spy and that Dreyfus was innocent.

A French magazine from 1899 features an image of Alfed Dreyfuss sitting mournfully in captivity on Devil's Island.

With this evidence, the public outcry grew even louder. One of the most eloquent voices of protest belonged to famous novelist Emile Zola. In 1898, Zola published a letter, called "I Accuse," which fiercely criticized the French military and government. Zola himself was convicted of **libel** and sentenced to a year in prison, although he escaped to England. Zola's involvement brought international attention to the Dreyfus Affair, and there was a retrial in 1899. Dreyfus was found guilty again, but within 10 days—after a new French government was elected—the sentence was overturned and Dreyfus was restored to his original rank. The case also prompted the French National Assembly to remove the last privileges the Catholic Church held in France.

"I have one passion only, for light, in the name of humanity which has borne so much and has a right to happiness. My burning protest is only the cry of my soul. Let them dare, then, to carry me to the court of appeals, and let there be an **inquest** in the full light of day!"

The conclusion of Emile Zola's famous "I Accuse" letter, January 1898.

Daniel O'Connell

Daniel O'Connell (1775–1847) was an Irishman who intended to overturn the ban on Catholics being elected to Parliament, where all laws relating to Britain and Ireland were made. O'Connell studied in France and then in Ireland, where he qualified as a lawyer in 1798. In 1823, O'Connell established the Catholic Association, which gained enormous support, especially in Ireland. Six years of intensive campaigning—including a number of public speeches attracting nearly a million people—helped the cause. In 1829, Parliament passed the Catholic Emancipation Act, overturning the previous ban on Catholic participation in Parliament. O'Connell was elected to Parliament that same year and represented Irish—and Catholic—interests as a Member of Parliament (MP) until his death.

"Brother, you say there is but one way to worship and serve the Great Spirit. If there is but one religion, why do you white people differ so much about it?"

Sagoyewatha, chief of the Native American Seneca tribe, referring to Christian missionaries who he believed were destroying traditional Native American religion.

The Indian Mutiny

The 19th century was the high point of European **colonialism**. Major powers such as Great Britain and France conquered large parts of Africa and Asia and established colonies, which were ruled from London, Paris, or other European capitals. The Europeans justified their control of these areas by saying that they brought modern ideas of government, justice, education, and health to "backward" regions.

But ancient cultures, along with established religions, already existed in many of these colonies. Europeans had gradually come to terms with religious toleration within their own boundaries (usually extending to different Christian groups and possibly to Jewish believers). Having to rule lands with large populations of Muslims, Hindus, and Buddhists was unfamiliar.

The British had to deal with a full-scale rebellion in India because they could not understand the religious needs of the local people. In 1857, the British issued new rifles to Indian soldiers. Riflemen had to bite off the end of greased cartridges in order to load the weapons. Rumors spread that the cartridges were greased with fat from either pigs or cows. Muslims believe pigs are unclean, and Hindus believe cows are sacred, so both groups were outraged. Beginning in May 1857, Indian soldiers rebelled across north and central India, leading to fierce fighting against the British. The mutiny, as the rebellion was called, was finally crushed in 1859. But the British had learned a difficult lesson about the heartfelt beliefs of people with different traditions.

Several influential leaders of the Indian Mutiny were executed by being tied to cannons, which were then shot.

Understanding and Tragedy

By the early 20th century, most Western countries provided some form of religious liberty for their citizens. Believers were free to worship as they chose, provided that their beliefs and worship did not break the laws of their country. This increased freedom had parallels in other freedoms that came after long struggles—racial equality, women's right to vote, freedom to form labor unions, and many others. It seemed to be a mark of a modern, civilized society to ensure the basic rights of as many people as possible.

Religious leaders from many faiths around the world had begun to meet at international conferences at the end of the 19th century. Representatives of Eastern religions, including Hindus, Buddhists, Sikhs, and Muslims, exchanged views with Christians and Jews at the Chicago Parliament of Religion in 1893. Similar gatherings at international expositions helped build mutual

The Chicago Parliament of the World's Religions was a key step toward religious freedom around the world. Participants stressed that no religion should be forced to sacrifice its beliefs.

understanding. Thus, respect for other people's beliefs began to replace ignorance and hatred, making people feel optimistic about the new century.

Prominent representatives of the League of Nations are shown in this photograph taken at San Remo, Italy, in May 1920. The League was created to prevent future world wars.

Unfulfilled Promise

Many people even saw the end of World War I (1914–18), the first conflict in which millions of people died, as a chance to build a new, fairer world. They believed that "old-fashioned" ideas of intolerance and warfare would be replaced with peaceful notions of cooperation and discussion. These hopes for peace led to the formation of the League of Nations—a forerunner of the United Nations (UN)—in 1920. The League had some immediate successes, particularly in its handling of the millions of European refugees who had fled from their countries during the war.

However, the League of Nations was powerless to curb the behavior of some of its members, especially Germany and the **Soviet Union**. These two

An anti-Semitic Nazi poster from 1933 reads: "Do you wish to be free [from Jewish domination]? Then vote the Nationalist Block!."

Thirteen-year-old Vera Berger was starving and seriously ill when Allied troops rescued her from the Belsen concentration camp in 1945.

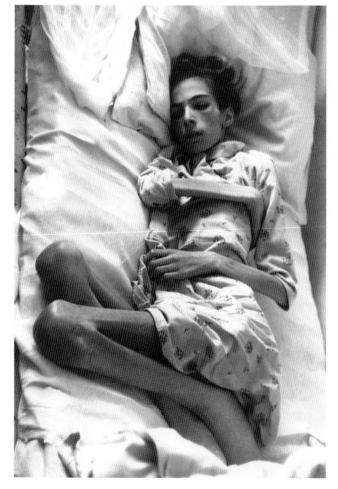

countries, among the most powerful in the world, were developing political systems that called for ruthless control at home and military action against countries with differing ideas.

By the early 1940s, Germany and the Soviet Union were on opposing sides in World War II (1939–45), the worst conflict in human history. Millions of people died before Germany and its allies were defeated in 1945. Only then did the outside world learn the true extent of the terrible **Holocaust** (see page 33), in which millions of Jews had been executed. After the war, Germany spent decades trying to come to terms with the violence that its people had witnessed and often approved. The Soviet Union retained its **communist** system and, with it, the severe restrictions on believers of any faith. Real change came in the 1980s when reforming leaders such as Mikhail Gorbachev included increased religious freedom among the changes they put in place in the Soviet Union.

The Holocaust

Adolf Hitler and his National Socialist (Nazi) Party believed in a strong Germany ruled by Aryan people. Aryans, according to the Nazis, were Northern European people who were "pure" Germans. Other German groups, in their view, only weakened Germany. "Others" was a very broad term that included homosexuals, Roma (Gypsy) people, and **Slavs**. But the group that Nazis hated most was Germany's Jewish population. Posters and books accused Jews of being cruel and miserly and of uniting with foreign forces that sought to crush Germany.

Throughout the 1930s, Nazi laws began to place restrictions on the lives of German Jews. They were denied the best education and jobs, and many were forced from their homes and businesses. After World War II began in 1939, Jews became the target of wide-scale attacks in Germany and in the countries that Germany conquered. Jews were rounded up and sent to concentration camps, where they awaited what the Nazis described as the "final solution" to Germany's problems—extermination of the Jewish population. By the end of World War II in 1945, as many as six million Jewish people had died in Nazi concentration camps. This tragic episode—one of the most murderous in human history—is known as the Holocaust. It revealed the depths to which human beings could sink when they based their lives on religious intolerance.

Jewish prisoners liberated from concentration camps in 1944 are shown wearing the Star of David, which the Nazis required all Jewish prisoners to wear.

A Voice Against the Nazis

The Reverend Martin Niemöller (1892–1984) had been a German submarine commander during World War I. In 1924, he became a Lutheran minister. Beginning in 1931, he served at a church in Berlin, where he saw the Nazi Party's actions firsthand. At first, Niemöller believed the Nazis to be German patriots, but he changed his mind when their policies began to persecute minorities, especially Germany's Jewish population. His opposition grew after he organized the Confessing Church, a group of Christians that publicly opposed Hitler's actions. Niemöller was arrested by the German secret police in 1937 and sent to concentration camps, where he remained until the end of World War II in 1945. His actions continue to inspire those who cherish religious freedom.

"In Germany they first came for the Communists—and I didn't speak up because I wasn't a Communist. Then they came for the Jews—and I didn't speak up because I wasn't a Jew. Then they came for the trade unionists— and I didn't speak up because I wasn't a trade unionist. Then they came for the Catholics—and I didn't speak up because I was a Protestant. Then they came for me—and by that time no one was left to speak up."

Reverend Martin Niemöller, who spent seven years in concentration camps because of his support for Germany's Jews.

Reverend Martin Niemöller, shown here in Chichester, England, in 1949, became a leading member of the World Council of Churches after World War II.

Early Warning

The Russian Revolution created the communist government of the Soviet Union in 1917. Although the new Soviet Constitution guaranteed many human rights, including religious liberty, in practice things worked differently. Churches, synagogues, and mosques were closed, and many religious leaders were sent to prison or to the harsh wilderness of Siberia. The worst religious persecution took place in the 1930s, under the brutal leadership of Joseph Stalin.

But as early as 1918, some Russian religious leaders were speaking out against the behavior of the Soviet government. Tikhon, the Russian Orthodox leader of Moscow and All Russia, issued a courageous call to faithful members of the Russian Orthodox Church on February 1, 1918. He accused the new Soviet government, which claimed to be the hero of the ordinary people, of cruelty and dishonesty. He then turned to his fellow Orthodox believers: "The enemies of the church seize power over it and its property by force of arms—oppose them with the force of your faith, a mighty cry of the whole people which will halt the madmen and show them that they have no right to call themselves the champions of the people's good."

Soviet leader Joseph Stalin, shown here in 1937, had actually studied briefly to be a Russian Orthodox priest before becoming an enemy of religion.

Taking Liberties?

In most cases, worshipers have no trouble balancing their religious beliefs with the laws of their country. Nevertheless, over the years, many conflicts have arisen when there have been clashes between people's religious beliefs and the laws established by their government.

U.S. law, for example, states that a person can be married to only one person at a time. But soon after the founding of the Mormon faith in the 19th century, this law against polygamy was tested. Mormon men were urged to take more than one wife—and to have many children—as a way of building numbers.

A Mormon man poses with his six wives and one child outside their Utah home in 1885.

Muhammad Ali

Boxer Muhammad Ali (1942–), known as "the Greatest," is one of the world's most admired sportsmen. He is a symbol of courage and determination and won an Olympic gold medal for the U.S. in 1960. But at one time, Ali's religious beliefs put him at odds with both his country and boxing authorities. Boxing as Cassius Clay (his original name), he won the heavyweight world title in 1964. That same year, he converted to Islam, changing his name to Muhammad Ali. Three years later, Ali refused to be **inducted** into the U.S. Army because his Muslim beliefs made him a **conscientious objector**. Ali was convicted of draft evasion, or refusing to join the armed forces when called, and the ruling bodies of boxing took away his heavyweight title. Ali eventually returned to boxing while the legal battle to regain his title continued. Finally, in 1971, the U.S. Supreme Court overturned Ali's conviction, and he was free to contend for the world title once more.

Even as world champion, Muhammad Ali struggled to retain his right to fight in the mid-1960s because of his religious and political views.

Other denominations have had clashes with governments. **Rastafarians**, for example, believe that marijuana is a necessary part of their religious ceremonies. The Jehovah's Witnesses profess allegiance only to Jesus Christ and refuse to salute any flag or to serve in the armed forces. Christian Scientists believe that prayer alone can cure people of illnesses. Many Christian Scientists refuse medical treatment, even in emergencies. This decision, especially if it involves a sick child, has often placed Christian Scientists in conflict with the law.

Defining a Religion

Scientology is a religion founded by American science-fiction writer L. Ron Hubbard in 1954. It is based on dianetics, a type of psychological treatment. Using dianetics, people confront painful memories in order to achieve mental health. In order to do this, though, believers must pay money to officials of the Church of Scientology. If this process took place in a medical setting, the people doing the treatment would have to pay tax on the money they received. But since the Church of Scientology is officially classified as a religion, it pays no tax to the U.S. government. Some former Scientologists claim that Hubbard organized Scientology as a religion solely in order to escape paying tax in countries such as the United States. Other countries have been slow to recognize Scientology as a religion for this reason.

French Scientologists defend their religion in a 1999 protest after the French justice minister proposed banning the organization.

A Jamaican Rastafarian lights up a marijuana cigarette in what he considers to be a religious ceremony.

A Writer's Death Sentence

Indian-born novelist Salman Rushdie (1947–) has written award-winning novels, short stories, children's fiction, and travel books since 1974. None of his works is as famous—or infamous—as his 1988 novel *The Satanic Verses*. This mixture of comedy, fantasy, and philosophy was widely praised, but it also provoked an outcry among many Muslims around the world. These people believed that Rushdie, who himself is a Muslim, was attacking the Islamic faith and its holy book, the Koran. Five countries banned the book as soon as it was published. In 1989, things took an even more serious turn. Iran's spiritual leader, Ayatollah Ruholla Khomeini, declared that Rushdie and everyone else involved in the book's publication should be put to death. Khomeini's followers offered a bounty of up to $5 million to anyone who would kill them. The bounty remained in place even after Rushdie apologized and reaffirmed his Islamic faith, so for several years the author had to remain in hiding. From 1995 onward, Rushdie began to appear more often in public, but the death threat remains.

Finding a Balance

It is difficult for governments and courts to preserve religious liberty while at the same time ensuring that basic laws and justice are also protected. Some countries, such as Singapore and Trinidad and Tobago (see page 41), must acknowledge a wide variety of beliefs even within a small population. And then there is the problem of deciding whether an organization can really call itself a religion—and therefore qualify for protection and other benefits, including not having to pay taxes.

Under God?

Many American schoolchildren recite the Pledge of Allegiance each day. The Pledge is so familiar to most Americans that they might not realize that it is surrounded by controversy. The heart of this controversy lies in the words "under God." These words do not appear in the original version of the Pledge, written by Francis Bellamy in 1892. Bellamy's version read simply: "I pledge allegiance to my Flag and the Republic for which it stands, one nation, indivisible, with liberty and justice for all."

The words "my Flag" were changed to "the Flag of the United States of America" in 1924. Few Americans disagreed with that change, but 30 years later, the words "under God" were added after the phrase "one nation." The later change was to contrast the United States (with its religious traditions) with the **atheistic** Soviet Union, which was seen as America's greatest rival and enemy. Many Americans, however, believed that because religion and government are separate under U.S. law, there should be no mention of God in the Pledge.

On June 26, 2002, a three-judge panel of the 9th U.S. Circuit Court of Appeals voted two to one that the Pledge is unconstitutional because of the phrase. The decision affects only nine states, mainly in the West, and it will take effect only if it is upheld on appeal. Even that might not be the end of the story. Supporters or opponents of the "under God" phrase could take the case to the U.S. Supreme Court, which has the final say in interpreting the U.S. Constitution. Only then would there be a decision that would affect all 50 states regarding whether to keep or eliminate the phrase "under God."

Celebrating Diversity

The two-island Caribbean country of Trinidad and Tobago has a population that comes from many different backgrounds. Trinidadians can trace their descent from European settlers, African slaves, and farm workers brought from India. The religions these people follow are equally varied, including many Christian denominations, as well as Islam, Hinduism, and Judaism. But rather than becoming a source of conflict, this mixture of religions has added to the friendly atmosphere of the country.

The major festivals of each religion are public holidays for all Trinidadians. Many citizens learn about their neighbors' different faiths by sharing in their celebrations. The most famous of these festivals is Carnival, a lively celebration that precedes the Christian season of Lent. Every year, Trinidadians celebrate the following other Christian-based holidays: Spiritual Baptist Liberation Shouter Day, Good Friday, Easter Monday, Corpus Christi, Christmas Day, and Boxing Day. In addition, there are also days off for the Hindu festival of Divali and the Muslim festival of Eid al-Fitr.

Trinidadian boys in colorful costumes join a parade as part of the country's annual Carnival celebration.

New Challenges

The world is constantly changing, and so too are the complex problems surrounding the campaign to promote and maintain religious freedom. Civil wars and regional fighting in places such as Sudan, Nigeria, and the Asian island of East Timor have led to cruel attacks on religious minorities. Many of the newly independent countries that once formed part of the Soviet Union have shown little respect for religious freedom.

A World Response

Most of the world community accepts that religious freedom is one of the basic human rights that all people should enjoy. These rights form the basis of the United Nations, which has helped establish guidelines to safeguard basic human rights—including freedom of religion—in its member countries. The UN is also responsible for supplying money and other economic assistance to

developing countries. Knowing that this important aid might stop if human rights are not preserved has convinced many governments to support religious freedom. When this isn't enough, the UN sometimes sends peacekeepers to world trouble spots in order to restore these rights.

Other military actions have been based on similar goals. The U.S.-led force that invaded Afghanistan in 2001 and 2002 aimed to overthrow the Taliban government in that country. The Taliban had offered support and training for the terrorists who planned the "9/11" attacks in 2001. It had also imposed harsh religious restrictions on the Afghan population—restrictions that went far beyond the Islamic principles that the Taliban claimed to support. Since the defeat of the Taliban, Afghanistan remains a poor and sometimes dangerous country, but its people are grateful to be able to exercise their religious rights more freely.

Other victories are less clear-cut. Another U.S.-led force defeated the forces of Iraqi dictator Saddam Hussein in 2003. The following years, however, have shown some of the difficulties of trying to establish a democratic government to replace him. Iraq has two rival Muslim populations—the Sunni and the Shiite—as well as a smaller Christian community. Observers worry that having one group in power could lead to harsh treatment of Iraq's other religious groups.

Pakistani Shiite Muslims, who are in the minority, demonstrate against the religious violence of Sunni Muslims in 2004.

Religious Freedom Watchdogs

With the spread of modern communications, especially the Internet, it has become easier to keep track of religious freedom around the world. A number of organizations—many of them also involved in monitoring wider human rights issues—receive reports from countries where this freedom is threatened. Some of these organizations, such as Amnesty International, are able to collect information from all over the world. They have the resources and support to mount international campaigns to promote human rights. Other organizations are devoted to keeping track of events in a particular country or region. For example, the Sudan Infonet Web site provides information about the Sudanese conflict, which has seen Christian communities coming under attack from Muslim forces loyal to the government. All of these watchdog organizations can pass on accounts of the worst abuses of religious freedom to governments and to the United Nations, which can then put pressure on the countries where religious freedom is threatened.

The New Century

The new century has also brought with it new challenges created by technology. While new types of communication, including radio, television, and the Internet, allow religious leaders to spread their message and to reach loyal believers, they can also be misused by people aiming to make money or to trick believers—all in the name of religion. Governments today must closely monitor the work of "televangelists," or religious spokesmen who use television to reach wide audiences. Most of these people are sincere believers who ask for support from their viewers only to help spread their message. Others, however, take advantage of those who are unwell or fearful in order to make money for themselves.

Likewise, the Internet has helped spread knowledge about human rights and religious kindness, but it has also allowed bigots to send out messages of hate and violence aimed at some religious communities. Thus, the fight for religious freedom, which began hundreds of years ago, must continue today, both to establish basic freedoms in places where they are still denied and to deal with new challenges in countries that have a strong tradition of protecting those freedoms.

Whose Rights?

Sometimes, what some people consider to be a political issue is also a matter of religious principle to others. The controversy surrounding **abortion** is a good example, especially in the United States. Many **feminists** and their supporters believe that a woman should have control over her body and the **fetus** she carries while she is pregnant. Opponents of abortion believe that the fetus is another human being and that an abortion kills that other person. The controversy has become even more complicated because certain religious groups, especially the Catholic Church and some Protestant denominations, have become involved. For them, abortion violates one of their basic religious beliefs—not to murder. It is hard to find any middle ground between these two positions. Many American voters decide on their political candidates on the basis of this single issue.

Backlash Against Islam

The terrible events of September 11, 2001, when terrorists steered passenger planes into the Twin Towers in New York City and the Pentagon in Washington, D.C., have had profound consequences on religious freedom around the world. Some people believe that because one group of Muslims carried out this attack, all Muslims are supporters of terrorism. In the months following "9/11," mosques and Islamic community centers were attacked in the United States, Great Britain, France, and other countries. Islamic leaders, many of whom have constantly preached peace and toleration among religious faiths, received threatening letters that spoke of violent revenge.

Western countries with large Muslim populations have found it difficult to defuse the anti-Muslim

feelings of some of their citizens while at the same time preserving the freedom of Muslim citizens to continue with their beliefs. The position in France (which has a large Muslim community) is a case in point. In February 2004, the French government passed a law outlawing many religious symbols from French public schools. Although the law prohibits large Christian crosses, Jewish skullcaps, and Sikh turbans, many people see it as being aimed squarely at Muslims. Nearly everyone refers to this law as the "headscarf law," since it bans the wearing of headscarves by Muslim girls. The government believes that by removing all of these symbols from schools, no child will become an easy target for bullies. But most people in the French Muslim community believe that the move is intended to attack one of the basic symbols of Muslim pride and identity.

Glossary and Suggested Reading

abortion   a medical operation to end a pregnancy

Anglicans   members of the Church of England

anti-Semitic   characterized by discrimination or hostility toward Jewish people

atheistic   not believing in God

Buddhism   religion founded by the Indian mystic Buddha (c. 563–483 B.C.)

colonialism   conquering other parts of the world and ruling them from the home country

communist   a type of government in which the state (government) owns all properties

Confucianism   A set of beliefs based on the teachings of the Chinese philosopher Confucius (551–479 B.C.)

conscientious objector   someone who refuses to fight in a war because of his or her beliefs

constitutions   systems of principles defining how a country or organization operates

converts   people who change their beliefs from one religion to another

Crusades   Christian military expeditions that aimed to seize the Holy Land from Muslims

denominations   organized groups of people sharing religious beliefs

Dissenters   people who disagreed with the beliefs and practices of the Church of England.

feminists   people who strongly support the rights of women

fetus   the unborn young of a human being or mammal

heresies   beliefs or practices that differ from an established religion

heretics   people who support a belief that others consider to be a heresy

Holocaust   a term describing the systematic persecution and murder of Jews and other groups by the Nazi government of Germany in the 1930s and 1940s

inducted   legally called upon to join the armed forces

Industrial Revolution   a period in the 18th and 19th centuries when there were rapid advances in manufacturing techniques

inquest   a public investigation, usually held before a jury

Islam   a religion that believes in one God, whose words were passed on to Muhammad

libel   a crime consisting of publishing untruths about someone or something

Middle Ages   a long period of European history, from the 5th to the 15th centuries

Muslims   people who believe in Islam

persecution   treating people badly because of their race, religion, or other beliefs

Puritans   English religious protestors who wanted to purify the Church of England

Rastafarians   members of a religion that celebrates black people's links with Africa.

ravishing   seizing or carrying away by force

Reformation   the period beginning in the early 16th century, when some people sought to change (reform) the beliefs and practices of the Catholic Church

revolutions   violent overthrow of countries or political systems

Separatists   English Christians who wanted a complete split from the Church of England

Shinto   a Japanese religion that features worship of nature and ancestors

Slavs   members of a group of Eastern European peoples (including Russians, Poles, and Czechs) who speak similar languages

Soviet Union   the name of a communist country that included Russia and 14 other neighbors from 1917 to 1991

statute   a law passed by an elected group such as a congress or parliament

Thirty Years' War   a European war (1618–48) between rival Christian groups

treason   betraying one's country, especially by helping that country's enemy

uniformity   always the same and not changing

Suggested Reading

Currie, Stephen. *Escapes from Religious Oppression*. San Diego: Lucent Books, 2003.

Dudley, William, ed. *Religion in America.* San Diego: Gale/Greenhaven, 2001.

Farish, Leah. *The First Amendment: Freedom of Speech, Religion, and the Press*. Berkely Heights, New Jersey: Enslow, 1998.

Weitzman, E., and L. Stuart. *I Am Jewish American*. New York: PowerKids Press, 1998.

Web Sites

Amnesty International
http://www.amnesty.org
Freedom House
http://www.freedomhouse.org
International Coalition for Religious Freedom
http://www.religiousfreedom.com/rfcom.htm
Sudan Infonet
http://sudaninfonet.tripod.com/NSI

Index